"There is more power in the real you than you can imagine!
Surprise yourself."
-JoAnn Corley

By
JoAnn R. Corley

This is the complementary workbook to my live workshop. It's also the first of its kind that has a corresponding YouTube Playlist.

www.joanncorley.com

ISBN: 9798878547178

For bulk orders use this email:
joann@joanncorley.com

Contents - Workbook Sections

~~~~~~

(This layout reflects your Career Portfolio set up)
~~~~~~

This page is for your *customized*

"table of contents" for easy access to key pages.

This is not only a guide, but a workbook.

The outside margins are slightly larger.

Mark it up – take notes – do the exercises.

| Introduction |

Welcome to "The Real You @Work: A Jumpstart Guide for Career Planning & Management to Unlock Your Career Potential"! In today's fast-paced and ever-evolving professional landscape, the key to success lies not only in your technical skills or qualifications but also in your ability to harness your authentic self to drive your career forward. And, it's ultimately about finding fulfillment, satisfaction, and growth in your career while staying true to yourself.

This handbook is designed as your roadmap to unlocking and leveraging the real you and all its potential so you can flourish in your professional endeavors. Whether you're just starting out in your career or are a seasoned professional looking to reignite your passion, the principles, insights, and strategies within these pages will empower you to identify what it takes to be at your best and maintain satisfaction in your work as you navigate the complexities of the ever-changing workplace with confidence and purpose.

Throughout this guide, you'll embark on a journey of self-discovery, exploring your distinct strengths, values, passions, and ambitions. You'll learn how to align your personal and professional identities, leverage your individuality, harness your natural talents, and cultivate a mindset that fosters ownership, growth and resilience in the face of challenges.

"The Real You at Work" provides you with practical tools, exercises actionable advice, and real-world examples to help you unlock your full potential, so you can thrive in any professional setting. This handbook builds the foundation of your Career Portfolio.

As you embark on this journey, remember that identifying "the real you" is not a destination but a continuous process of self-awareness, growth, and adaptation. And, it's beyond achieving external markers of success. It's also about finding, joy, meaning and fulfillment in the work you do and the impact you make. Embrace your uniqueness, trust in your abilities, and dare to unleash the real you in every aspect of your career.

So, are you ready to embark on this empowering quest to unlock your career potential as you become the best version of yourself at work? Let's dive in and discover the real you!

Food for Thought.

No matter what you do…
You can and do matter.
Do you believe that?

YOU make an impact – whether you see it or not.
You produce value…whether you see it or not!

So…if this is true
You might as well see it clearly, plan it thoughtfully, do it intentionally
and really make it count!

A Story

The great fire of 1666 destroyed the central part of London and laid a large number of its churches in ruins. It completely gutted the old St. Paul's and made necessary the building of the present noble cathedral. This was the opportunity for Sir Christopher Wren, to whom London owes very much for what is finest in its architecture and especially in the character of its central churches. He received for his compensation a salary less than that of the American unskilled worker, but as his epitaph truly says, his work was "not for himself but for the public good," and will keep bright his fame forever.

One morning he passed amoung the workmen, most of whom did not know him, and of three different men engaged in the same kind of work he asked the same question: "What are you doing?" From the first he received the answer: "I am cutting this stone.' From the second the answer was: "I am earning three shillings and six pence a day." But the third man straightened up, squared his shoulders, and holding his mallet in one hand and chisel in the other, proudly replied: "I am helping Sir Christopher Wren to build this great cathedral."

These are the three ways of looking at life & work:

1. I am just cutting this stone.

2. I am only earning a living.

3. I am doing a small part of a great work.

I have not seen the Architect and I do not altogether understand the plan. But I believe there *is* a plan, so I work with good spirit in which is no fear.

Source: Bruce Barton, "What Can A Man Believe,"

The Real You @Work – Planning to Work at Your Best

Most folks rarely engage in active career planning and even fewer know how to skillfully manage it. And, yet there are a few lucky enough to stumble upon supreme career success.

But for most, stumbling upon hasn't worked yet. You may be one of those who is ready for a Plan B.

Plan Be is deliberate. It's strategic. With guide in hand, it involves thoughtful discovery, planning, execution *and* management. That's the purpose of this resource – to get you started, doing all four.

It's also the first of its kind that has a complementary YouTube playlist to enhance your experience with the content.

Laying the Foundation

What to Expect

The intent of this guide is to provide you with the *simplest*, quickest approach and tools to jumpstart your quest. It is not meant to house all the information needed. So, I'll be recommending books and other resources for elements of planning for which you'd like to do a deeper dive.

The layout of the guide is designed to be an interactive handbook. You'll learn simple concepts one at a time and you'll take action on that concept through an exercise or series of exercises.

Ultimately, the purpose of this interactive guide is to assist you in constructing a first draft, core *framework* for a **Career Portfolio.** Part 1 of the handbook suggests what to include. Part 2 will address active career management.

More Than a Resume

What's a Career Portfolio?

A career portfolio is an ongoing **collection of everything related to your work experience**. It is a record of the work you've done including achievements, highlights, skills developed, knowledge acquired, certifications, awards & recognitions, comments from clients and colleagues, special projects outside the scope of your job description, volunteer work, special talents and even hobbies. In essence, anything that captures <u>all of who you are,</u> what you have and want to contribute to the world of work.

"How silly to think we can adequately represent the BEST of who are and what we have to contribute from a spotty memory on a page or two of a resume!"

What's Included in a Career Portfolio?

In its basic form, your Career Portfolio should include at least these 4 sections:

Part A: Career Planning…

- ✓ Your Personal Profile
- ✓ Your Professional Profile
- ✓ Your Work History

Part B: Career Management…

- ✓ Your Performance Tracker

Your Most Important Resource

Though you may have purchased this resource, please know the most valuable resource for your career planning and management is free! What's that? **It's you**!

The best guide and most important resource for planning **is <u>within</u> you**. It includes your internal guidance system and all the memories housed in your subconscious. It is this internal guidance that provides the critical planning information through cues and messages about what you are experiencing related to your work-life. This includes tasks, functions, responsibilities, atmosphere, relationships, company and even industry.

As you are working through-out your day, here's what cues and messages you want to tune-in to:

- ✓ what's meaningful
- ✓ what's satisfying
- ✓ what gives you energy
- ✓ what's gives you joy
- ✓ what easiest to do
- ✓ what's most natural
- ✓ what's annoying
- ✓ what you have to "force" yourself to do
- ✓ enjoy the least
- ✓ qualities of team, people, company, industry
- ✓ what you're contributing, accomplishing
- ✓ how you can quantify these in $ % #s

The key to leveraging this information is to collect and *document* it in real-time, rather than periodically relying on your memory for sporadic performance reviews or when you're in a job search and constructing a resume.

So much is missed with that approach. Plus, constructing a resume doesn't ask you to identify what you really enjoy - what gives you satisfaction. It's more about what you've done and what skills you possess.

> I believe the ultimate key to career success is *being clear & certain* about what you do exceptionally well as well as what energizes you and gives you satisfaction.

To start effective career planning and management, you'll need to begin a **career / work journal** that captures, and from which helps you construct your **internal profile**.

Your internal profile comprises who you are - how you're wired on the inside. Then you consider - in the contest of work - how all this is best expressed using skills, capabilities, aptitudes, natural talents, values and interests.

For a reference to how all this played out in my life, check my Kindle short – *The Force Within.*

Key Point:

Your most important planning asset is your level of self-awareness.

Your Internal Guidance

I discovered early on that having the most satisfying life you can is to be true to yourself. This also applies to what jobs you choose. You want to be able to choose jobs that *most closely match* **the true you** – those that are the most *natural* fit. Typically, those are the jobs that feel almost effortless – perhaps don't feel so much like "work" - and from which you experience the most satisfaction.

But, to achieve this, you have to:

> know the "true you" first,

> articulate that to yourself (the role of the journal) so you can

> effectively articulate it to others – verbally (interview) and in writing (resume).

A Natural Fit

Take my friend Sue. Many years ago, we were having a discussion about her feeling a need for a change from her current work, which at the time was teaching. Since my career planning philosophy was when considering a change, examine your everyday life and look for things you do naturally. One thing we identified is that within our group of friends, she was always the "go-to" person when someone needed to talk through an issue or needed a listening ear. She was warm, approachable, kind and empathetic. She was a natural at being a good listener and being the place folks could express what was in their head and heart. Her obvious career move?... counseling. That was twenty something years ago. Sue has had a highly successful counseling practice and has served many a head and heart.

Now, even though as a career coach I was available to help Sue sort through her cues, everyone has within them their own career guide and coach regularly providing cues and messages… if only we would just tune in, pay attention and take them seriously!

2 Items of Note About Fit

1. One additional consideration when thinking about fit is the connection between fit and personal power.

The better the job fit, the more "empowered" you feel. Fit gives you energy because you are connecting to the things that "turn you on" –how you're naturally wired. Connecting to your wiring turns on your energy and fuels your power, while feeding your ability and willingness to act stimulates desire. Desire is the origin of motivation (having a motive). Also, connecting with desire feeds satisfaction.

So, the better the fit, the easier the job – the less effort it takes. Jobs that are not a great fit typically take much more effort and are less satisfying.

I remember the first time I got a taste of running a company. I felt as if I was "running on all cylinders" as I described it. Every part of me was turned on. I felt fully alive, fully connected and engaged.

Insight

There are 2 kinds of work-related tired. Tired from working hard at something you love or enjoy. That's a satisfying kind of tire. And then, there is a tired from a job being exhausting because it takes so much out of you to do it.

2. For some there may not ever be "the perfect" fit job. So, the goal would be to prioritize what's most important, most satisfying, most energizing and then find a job that fits the best. The best in this case would be what matches at least the top part of your list or the majority of your most important, most satisfying.

Resource Recommendation: ***The Force Within***

A few years ago, I was asked by a dear HR friend to contribute to a blog series entitled The Leading Ladies. That request resulted in this short booklet The Force Within.

Referencing the concepts shared so far, you could interchange force and power. This booklet shares my journey in recognizing my internal force and how that was practically expressed as my external voice through my work.

"

Decide who you are…then live it proudly and boldly.

"

Setting Up Your Portfolio

Whether digital or offline, here is the recommended set up:

My Career Portfolio

As mentioned earlier, your portfolio should include these 4 core sections:

- ✓ Your Personal Profiles
- ✓ Your Professional Profile
- ✓ Your Work History
- ✓ Your Performance Tracker

Included in your career portfolio should not only be **your journal** but your **core profile** which includes all your completed worksheets.

So, this guide now turns into a workbook. The layout of the pages is designed to be your initial exercises, though eventually these will become part of your formal portfolio based on the format you choose.

[Note: if you wish to have any of the worksheets in this handbook in a separate format, email me and I'll send you a master pdf: joann@joanncorley.com]

To set up your portfolio, below are the core categories. Remember, your preliminary work will contain what you're aware of right now. As you continue to use this guide *your profile and portfolio will evolve* based on the ongoing growth of your awareness and experience.

▶ Personal Mission

Purpose

Calling

Vision

Your through-line

▶ Attributes

- Natural Wiring

Personality

Work behavior preference

- Core Values
- Capabilities
- Skills
- Distinct Aptitude
- Workplace Values
- Achievements
- Professional commendations
- Professional Works: publications, articles, podcasts, videos, etc.
- Education (including certificates, continuing education)
- Professional Associations
- Hobbies & Interests

Anything else to add?

Notes

The Real You @Work

Section 1: Personal Section

Finding the Real You

- Personal Mission

  Purpose

  Calling

  Vision

  Your Through-line

- Attributes

- Natural Wiring

  Personality

- Core Values

- Hobbies Interests Volunteer Work

Section 1: Personal Section – Personal Mission

Let's Start With > Answering these questions…while I'm here, what am I designed to do or be?...

Do those questions resonate with you? It may or may not and that's ok. If it does, consider:

- ⇨ Do you have a sense of mission or purpose...even calling…like something inside you is tugging or compelling you to act in a certain direction, in certain ways?

- ⇨ Have you been moved to demonstrate or express certain kinds of activities or behaviors? Example: from a very young age, I acted as if I was a teacher. I felt compelled to teach. That's one way I *naturally* expressed my energy.

Personal Mission & How It Will Be Expressed

Purpose
Calling
Vision
Your Through-line

So, after some thought, I'll ask again, "Does any of the above resonate with you?" Don't get hung up on the words so much as the overall theme.

Have you thought to yourself, "There is a reason why I'm here." Perhaps at an earlier time in your life you did and over time it's been squelched or completely extinguished? *Example: Early on for me it was as simple as knowing I was here to help people.*

Perhaps you "saw" yourself being or doing a certain thing?

If you are not sure or have forgotten, the next exercise might help pull it all together with the theme of a **"through line".**

Notes: Thoughts on mission, purpose, calling

The Story of You - Finding Your Through-Line
Retrospective Exercise Identifying the Natural You

Introduction

Most of us, whenever we feel trapped or in need of change, can lose sight of who we really are and what we really want or wanted for our lives. Decisions we've made in our adult life to date may have served, in some cases, to sabotage the real us – that part of us, that when fed properly, provides us with a sense of **energy, purpose and joy**.

Your Beginnings
The purpose of this exercise is to recapture or recreate the dreams you had concerning your life and how you envisioned playing out your life based on your uniqueness and *natural* interest.

It is important to remember that as you work through this exercise it should be done in a "free-style" form. Do not place any judgements on any part of the exercise (e.g. the way you write, what you record, how extreme any part of the answer seems, whether or not it's realistic...etc.)

Recapturing is foundational to any productive and healthy life change. The key premise to this exercise is the belief that you are created with certain talents, interests, capabilities and dreams. How you have lived your life has either nurtured or suppressed them.

In your answers – you may begin to recognize "running themes" that define the true you. That is called **your through-line.** An essential question to consider as you review your answers is has that through-line been represented in the career decisions you've made to date.

To Begin

1. Find a quiet place.
2. Identify what you want to write with and on. I *highly* recommend you do this and many exercises in a hand-written format vs. typing. You want to fully leverage the neuroscience of handwriting. Writing by hand activates more parts of your brain than typing. (At the end of the workbook - see the bonus article on this subject.)
3. Initially block at least one hour. Do not expect to complete this exercise in one sitting. The more thorough and detailed *over time*, the better. You will notice that more thoughts will come to mind days later because you have given your subconscious permission to explore the areas where these thoughts reside and perhaps have been suppressed.

Consider your first attempts the primer…as if you are trying to prime a water pump at a well. Initially you get a few trickles, then at some point the water starts flowing.

This is how it will be with your memories. You are priming your subconscious where all your collective life experience is housed. You'll want to tap as much as possible to resurface the real, authentic you.

4. Begin with a simple breathing exercise to completely clear your mind. I suggest inhaling and exhaling each on a count of seven, three times. The flow of thought will come when you have a deep sense of calm. (Depending on your own state, you may need to do more than once.)

Note: You may notice a lot of "noise" in your mind at first. There may be a natural resistance to allowing yourself to connect with the deep parts that have gone unattended for so long. It may feel somewhat threatening because some of us have developed unconscious ways of suppressing these thoughts, areas of our lives or memories.

This is actually a natural form of emotional protection and therefore, you may experience some stress not only in an attempt to connect with unattended areas but also when you'll be asked to reconcile your deep desires with your present reality - if they do not match.

That's why - as you do these exercises - you are not to make any judgements or attempt any edits about your thoughts. The goal is just to get them out and recorded.

Note: The value of this exercise is in **your answers** not in the questions alone. The *quality of discovery* depends on your willingness to create the atmosphere and dynamic to allow it to happen; to release the real you!

Reminder: these questions will begin to stir up memories from your subconscious and as you continue to "sleep on them, new or expanded answers might percolate. Make sure and **record** those as well.

Why This Exercise?

It has been my belief over the years that what kids do in play – unedited in their early years - gives clues to what will play into their best, most satisfying career choices.

These answers also serve as the starting point of what is your **"through line"** which is a running narrative of how your authentic self has been expressed (hopefully consistently) at varying stages of your life.

"It takes courage to grow up to be who you really are."
- *EE Cummings*

Retrospective Questions:

When I was a young child, I loved......
(Sample Answer: games.> (continue thought with .... "what kind of games and why...etc.")

Playing:
Reading:
Pretending to be:

When I was in junior high and high school, my favorite activities were....
Because............

When I was in junior high and high school, my favorite subjects /classes were....
I enjoyed them because......

When I was in high school, my favorite extracurricular activities were...
I participated because...
In college, my favorite subjects were...

Because....

When I was a young child, I thought myself unique in the following ways...

When I was a young child, people said I was...

Said I should be...Said I would be...

When I was a young child, I wanted to be...

When I was in high school, I wanted to be...

When I was in college, I wanted to be...
In my collective work experience from high school until now, my favorite work experiences were.......

Because….

My least favorite was…

Because…

If I had no concerns about earning money for a living, I would do…

Because…

Do you currently carry any regrets of opportunities missed (related to any circumstances) or risks you should have taken in your life and why?

I have always dreamed of doing… (maybe one item or a list)

I have always dreamed of being………………

In 10 years, I *envision* my life as follows: (be as specific and descriptive as possible describing every aspect of your life, family, career home, hobbies, spiritual life, character, marriage.)

Summary
Ok, so what did you discover...remember? Could you begin to identify your through-line?

Summary Notes

Attributes

The next part of the personal section of your portfolio is your attributes – how you would best describe the true you…your personal qualities.

Defined: a quality or feature regarded as a characteristic or inherent part of someone or something.

If you were to ask those who know you best how they would describe you, what would they say?

How do *you* describe yourself? What words in the list provided *best* describe and represent you?

For this exercise, you'll be **going through the list twice**. Once to circle what resonates and second to drill down to those you consider to be your core qualities – that describe you best.

Select the core qualities from those circled with a checkmark. Also, the words are provided alphabetically to the left with room for notes on the right.

Note: This exercise is not only for your core portfolio, but also for interview preparation.

Tips:

- Please don't over analyze – respond to the words with your heart or energy more than with your head.

- Obviously, this is not an all-inclusive word list. If a word on this list prompts one that resonates better and is more meaningful, record that one and use it going forward. – own it!

Attributes: Personal Qualities

Source: https://simplicable.com/en/personal-attributes

Accepting	Accomplished
Achiever	Active
Adaptable	Adept
Ambitious	Analytical
Approachable	Artistic
Assertive	Attentive
Balanced	Calm
Candid	Capable
Careful	Caring
Cheerful	Collaborative
Committed	Communicative
Compassionate	Competent
Competitive	Confident
Conscientious	Considerate
Consistent	Cooperative
Courteous	Creative
Critical Thinker	Cultured
Customer-focused	Dedicated
Design Thinker	Detail-Oriented
Determined	Diligent
Diplomatic	Discreet
Driven	Dutiful
Effective	Efficient

Empathetic	Energetic
Enterprising	Enthusiastic
Established	Ethical
Experienced	Fair
Fast Learner	Flexible
Focused	Forgiving
Friendly	Generous
Giving	Good With Customers
Good with People	Good-humored
Grit	Grounded
Hard Working	Helpful
High Cultural Competence	Honest
Imaginative	Impartial
Independent	Influential
Intelligent	Introspective
Inventive	Judicious
Knowledgeable	Leader
Likeable	Logical
Loyal	Mature
Meticulous	Observant
Open-minded	Organized
Original	Outgoing
Passionate	Patient
People Person	Persistent

Personable	Polished
Polite	Positive
Pragmatic	Principled
Productive	Professional
Prudent	Punctual
Rational	Realistic
Reflective	Relationship Builder
Relaxed	Reliable
Renown	Reputable
Resilient	Resourceful
Respected	Respectful
Responsible	Risk Taker
Self-Directed	Self-Motivated
Self-Starter	Self-aware
Self-correcting	Serious
Sincere	Skilled
Social	Stable
Strong Work-Ethic	Sympathetic
Tactful	Talented
Tenacious	Thorough
Tolerant	Trustworthy
Understanding	Versatile
Warm	Well-Known
Well-mannered	Willing to Learn

Personal Wiring

Many professionals are familiar with and have even taken a personality "test". Though not tests as we know the word, they are assessments designed to give you a more tangible understanding of how your brain takes in information, processes and responds with a way of thinking (for example left brain vs. right) and responding behaviorally – what we say and do.

Our brains are wired to respond to life experiences in different ways with different *preferences.*

Most popular in the corporate world is Myers-Briggs. A cousin of that – not as well known – is the Keirsey model.

For team building, leadership & management development, I also use a simpler, less complex assessment (meaning has less dimensions) called the SELF profile.

For me Keirsey was extremely helpful and for this work is first choice. The assessment comes with a wonderful book entitled; *Please Understand Me.* If you'd like to take a personality assessment for career planning, this is the one I recommend:

Main Website: Link: https://www.keirsey.com/

Purchase book via Amazon: https://keirsey.com/publications/books/

I'm leaving the corresponding right page to record your findings and notes.

Notes

Personality – Notes…

Core Values
There are 2 ways to see values:

1> At your core – in your inner being - is a certain kind of orientation. You can even call it your spirit, which is *the source* of your energy. That source has certain characteristics that comprise that spirit/energy. Those characteristics are commonly known as values.

Values – those characteristics – each have an element of energy to it.

Now this may sound a bit weird, so hang with me here. Here's an example – have you ever experienced a quality in someone that was "sickening" to you? And if you were around it very much, it - in fact - could cause you to become physically sick?

Conversely, when you are around someone whose qualities you enjoy, you actually get energized whenever you are with them. For example, I'm really attracted to and enjoy being around someone who is calm enough to think something through under pressure, or someone who is so confident about who they are, I feel inspired by them. (Inspiration is a form of energy).

2> Values are also seen as something very meaningful to you, that really matter. These can be both tangible and intangible. For example, I value time. I also value candor.

Now consider the list provided. It may take several pass throughs.

1. Initially circle what clicks with you. Don't analyze, just respond to the words that you feel connected to.
2. Then choose what you would consider to be your top values, most important, couldn't function without.
3. You'll notice as you identify your values, there will be a desire range – say 1 to 5. If you had to choose or list in order, those that matter most to least. Try to order them as best you can. The list will come in handy whenever you are making decisions.

4. You should know that your core values are not only for your career choices, but also for your personal life – particularly in relationships. Knowing and holding to your values is a fundamental key to your happiness. What you value, gives you life!

Application Example

Decision-making: Choosing a company

I really value – I'm attracted to – innovation, improvement, creativity. I have worked for companies whose cultures were not like that. Honestly, it drove me nuts and I absolutely did not enjoy working for them.

So, another valuable reason to do this exercise is to ensure that when you decide to work for a company, a manager/leader, its values are as closely aligned to yours as much as possible.

When you are interviewing,
you'll want to explore this area with your own set of questions.

Additional Resource:
You may want to check out this link: https://www.scienceofpeople.com/core-values/
It gives a categorized approach to values that you may find helpful. For example, it has, values in life, values at work, values in relationships.

Let's start with this list…

Core Values – *What really matters to you personally…*

Source: https://thehappinessplanner.com/pages/list-of-core-values

Acceptance
Accomplishment
Accountability
Accuracy
Achievement
Adaptability
Alertness
Altruism
Ambition
Amusement
Assertiveness
Attentive
Awareness
Balance
Beauty
Boldness
Bravery
Brilliance
Calm
Candor
Capable
Careful
Certainty
Challenge
Charity
Cleanliness
Clear
Clever
Comfort
Commitment
Common sense
Communication
Community
Compassion
Competence
Concentration
Confidence
Connection
Consciousness
Consistency
Contentment
Contribution
Control
Conviction
Cooperation
Courage
Courtesy
Creation
Creativity
Credibility
Curiosity
Decisive
Decisiveness
Dedication
Dependability
Determination
Development
Devotion
Dignity
Discipline
Discovery
Drive
Effectiveness
Efficiency
Empathy
Empower
Endurance
Energy
Enjoyment
Enthusiasm
Equality
Ethical
Excellence
Experience
Exploration
Expressive
Fairness
Family
Famous
Fearless
Feelings
Ferocious
Fidelity
Focus
Foresight
Fortitude
Freedom
Friendship
Fun
Generosity
Genius
Giving
Goodness
Grace
Gratitude
Greatness
Growth
Happiness
Hard work
Harmony
Health
Honesty
Honor
Hope
Humility
Imagination
Improvement
Independence
Individuality
Innovation
Inquisitive
Insightful
Inspiring
Integrity
Intelligence
Intensity
Intuitive
Irreverent
Joy
Justice
Kindness
Knowledge
Lawful
Leadership
Learning
Liberty
Logic
Love
Loyalty
Mastery
Maturity
Meaning
Moderation
Motivation
Openness
Optimism
Order
Organization
Originality
Passion
Patience
Peace
Performance
Persistence
Playfulness
Poise
Potential
Power
Present
Productivity
Professionalism
Prosperity
Purpose
Quality
Realistic
Reason
Recognition
Recreation
Reflective
Respect
Responsibility
Restraint
Results-oriented
Reverence
Rigor
Risk
Satisfaction
Security
Self-reliance
Selfless
Sensitivity
Serenity
Service
Sharing
Significance
Silence
Simplicity
Sincerity
Skill
Skillfulness
Smart
Solitude
Spirit
Spirituality
Spontaneous
Stability
Status
Stewardship
Strength
Structure
Success
Support
Surprise
Sustainability
Talent
Teamwork
Temperance
Thankful
Thorough
Thoughtful
Timeliness
Tolerance
Toughness
Traditional
Tranquility
Transparency
Trust
Trustworthy
Truth
Understanding
Uniqueness
Unity
Valor
Victory
Vigor
Vision
Vitality
Wealth
Welcoming
Winning
Wisdom
Wonder

Core Values cont…

Hobbies / Interests

You never know how these can be incorporated into your career path or job search. They reflect a part of your that is unique and will set you apart.

Detail experiences and interests, activities, subjects -- many people take for granted skills and capabilities developed within these activities and therefore should be a part of your portfolio.

You want to make sure you bring everything to the table for consideration in assessing the opportunities for your next move and what you want to bring forward in your next role.

Life Experience (examine and record – roles and experiences)

Travel

Volunteering

Religious / spiritual organizations

Professional Organizations

Personal Achievements

Hobbies & Interests – cont…

The Real You @Work
Section 2: Professional Section

- Capabilities
- Skills
- Distinct Aptitude (e.g. industry specific)
- Workplace Values
- Achievements
- Professional commendations
- Professional Works: publications, articles, podcasts, videos, etc.
- Education (including certificates, continuing education)

Professional Section

Now we're moving into the professional section of your Career Portfolio. Let's start with the most popular elements for job descriptions, resumes, LinkedIn profiles and interviews. This should be an eye-opening segment. AS a former recruiter, professional development coach and HR professional, I have a lot to say here!

Capabilities, Skills, Aptitude & Talent

You might be kind of curious why these are listed together. I've done so because they are frequently confused and mis-used.

So, let's bring some clarity and it will also help you gain a broader understanding of what you enjoy, what you can offer and how to articulate that on resumes and in interviews.

Let's start with definitions and the one that's most commonly used:

***Skill* >** A skill is something one knows how to do *very well*. Consider it a "mastered behavior". You're able to do it so well, it feels effortless. Typically, you also feel good doing it because it provides a feeling of competence, which feeds your confidence and satisfaction.

A skill, in the context of work, is also a **job function** which typically appears in job descriptions.

So, what's a capability?

***Capability* >** A capability is something you have the capacity or ability to do but has not yet reached the level of a skill or mastery. Ex. I can shoot a basket. I am capable of that. Can I shoot like Michael Jordan…uh…no.

***Aptitude* >** a natural capacity or ability

The next consideration is Aptitude. To position yourself for career success, it's good to know what's *natural* for you to do. Some might use the phrase "have a knack for". Both aptitude and talent address the area of natural.

***Talent* > is** the ability to do something well that is innate. It's as if a certain level of **skill is natural**, displayed with no formal training. This even is on a range from natural propensity toward an advance skill of genius. Some even use the word "gifted".

Innate and natural really refer to the same orientation - *easy* to interact with. Whether it's information or an activity. Your brain or body just work in an easy way and can even feel effortless. Common in our dialogue, "That comes easy to me."

A great example of this is my stepdaughter who just has a natural, even fun relationship with Math. I admire her! On an advanced level, it's a struggle for me. Beyond algebra or geometry my brain had to work harder to work with and understand concepts.

Of note, talent can also be demonstrated at an early age. That's why the Retrospective exercise is important.

Now, this doesn't mean those with an innate talent don't need practice. Talent can be improved, expanded, cultivated and grown. For example, Michael Jordan was just a mediocre basketball player in high school and yet went on to become a basketball icon. Tiger Woods, though showing hints of talent at a very young age, is known for his dedicated practice; up early on the course practicing his swing and watching hours of tape.

Other Examples:

Think of any sport. Consider who are the best and why. The best is *the most* skilled, usually developed with much practice. *Other examples:*

Coaching in management. There are many who are capable of having a coaching conversation. Very few are effective and skilled.

Public speaking. You can find a slew of those who consider themselves professional speakers. There are few I would consider skilled or exceptional.

Pick just about any profession and this rings true. You hate to say it, but even in the world of medicine…some Doctors are better than others – though all graduated from Med school and some went on to become specialists.

So, what are your talents, skills and capabilities. Let's use the corresponding page to begin identifying these - particularly related to most job functions. I've laid them out in key categories. Here is the source link: https://www.indeed.com/career-advice/career-development/skills-list

How to Use

Just like the attributes exercise:

1. Go through each list and circle what resonates.
2. Then go back and mark which you're most capable of…
3. Have demonstrated a certain level of skill…
4. Finally, highlight which of these gives you the most satisfaction…what you *truly* enjoy...what turns you on!

To follow are behavioral capabilities / skills. There is also a section for capabilities and skills related to a specific industry and job type like coding, illustrating, typing which you'll need to fill in without prompts. Also, these lists are not meant to be all inclusive, please add as needed.

< Thinking Style >

Strategic

Synthesizing

Analysis

Observing

Problem-solving

Simplifying

Conceptual thinking

Evaluating

Streamlining

Creative thinking

Brainstorming

Cost-benefit analyzing

Deductive reasoning

Inductive reasoning

Assessing

Evidence collecting

Troubleshooting

Organizing

Planning

Envisioning

Diagnosing

Examining

< Working with Others >

Mentoring

Counseling

Advising

Developing

Managing

Directing

Supervising

Training

Teaching

Influencing

Supporting

Helping

Facilitator

Coordinator

< Language / Communicating >

Speaking

Writing

Conversing

Reinterpreting

Public speaking

Explaining

Rephrasing

Synthesizing concepts

Negotiator

Persuader

Visual expression/design

< Technical – Industry Related >

e.g. coding, accounting, creative, design, data analytics, AI

This section can also include proficiency of use …e.g. software

Summary Notes:

Side Bar |

One of the greatest heartaches I experience as a career and professional development coach is seeing folks stuck in careers in which they are not happy. **Life is just too short for that!** This comes from a faulty approach to career planning and management

It's common for people to pursue jobs based on a job description or title rather than *first* knowing the skills and job functions they enjoy using and which they are supremely competent and then looking to see and know that those are included *in a variety* of job descriptions.

In career planning it's essential to know - particularly in the knowledge worker area - that most skills and capabilities apply to many job types no matter the title. Think about this for a moment.

Because this is not recognized, people limit their job searches to job descriptions rather than to their skills capabilities and aptitudes that can be applied in a variety of job contexts.

This also means hiring managers limit the scope of appropriate candidates. There a way more "qualified" candidates than they think. This debunks the thinking of "finding the right or best candidate".

So, this section asks you to *first* identify your **base or core skills, capabilities and aptitudes** that serves as your career foundation. Then you can add on your *industry specific* knowledge – skills + experience.

Then when doing a job search you look for job types and descriptions that **first include** your core set => then industry=> then formal job description=> and finally job title.

Sometimes, depending on how jobs are posted you might have to go in reverse meaning job title first. But, make sure you are approaching your assessment of opportunities from your core first.

So, when building the professional section of your career portfolio that will then carry over into your job search, start with your core competencies (skills capabilities, aptitudes)=> then industry specific of the same => then look for related industries of other industries of interest => job types within those industries => job descriptions => job titles => companies.

This is another resource I wanted to share with more word/skill options.
Reminder – action verbs are behaviors. *Mastered* behaviors are skills.

Resume Action Verbs and Adverbs

Management/ Leadership Skills
administered
assigned
attained
chaired
consolidated
contracted
coordinated
delegated
developed
directed
eliminated
enhanced
enforced
established
evaluated
executed
generated
headed
hired
improved
incorporated
increased
inspected
instituted
managed
motivated
organized
oversaw
planned
presided
prioritized
produced
recommended
reorganized
reviewed
scheduled
strengthened
supervised

Communication Skills
addressed
advertised
arranged
collaborated
communicated
composed
condensed
contacted
convinced
corresponded
defined
directed
drafted
edited
elicited
explained
expressed
formulated
influenced
interpreted
interviewed
judged
lectured
marketed
mediated
moderated
negotiated
observed
participated
persuaded
presented
promoted
publicized
reconciled
recruited
referred
reported
resolved
responded
spoke
suggested
synthesized
translated
wrote

Research Skills
analyzed
clarified
collected
compared
conducted
determined
evaluated
examined
extracted
formulated
gathered
identified
interpreted
interviewed
invented
investigated
located
measured
organized
researched
reviewed
solved
summarized
surveyed
systematized
tested

Technical Skills
applied
assembled
built
calculated
conserved
constructed
designed
determined
developed
installed
maintained
operated
programmed
resolved
specialized
upgraded

Teaching Skills
adapted
advised
arranged
clarified
communicated
conducted
coordinated
critiqued
developed
enabled
evaluated
explained
facilitated
guided
individualized
instructed
motivated
set goals
stimulated
taught
trained
transmitted
tutored

Creative Skills
acted
composed
conceptualized
created
designed
directed
displayed
drew
entertained
fashioned
formulated
founded
illustrated
introduced
invented
modeled
originated
performed
photographed
planned
revised
shaped

Helping Skills
advocated
aided
answered
assisted
cared for
clarified
counseled
diagnosed
educated
encouraged
facilitated
familiarized
furthered
helped
influenced
insured
mentored
provided
referred
rehabilitated
resolved
simplified
supplied
supported
volunteered

Organizational Skills
approved
arranged
catalogued
categorized
charted
classified
coded
collected
compiled
corresponded
distributed
filed
generated
implemented
inspected
maintained
monitored
operated
organized
prepared
processed
provided
recorded
reviewed
scheduled
sorted
submitted
standardized
systemized
updated
validated
verified

Financial Skills
analyzed
appraised
audited
balanced
budgeted
calculated
computed
developed
estimated
forecasted
managed
marketed
planned
projected
reconciled
reduced
researched

More Verbs...
achieved
completed
contributed
effected
electrified
expanded
improved
navigated
negotiated
pioneered
perfected
promoted
quoted
reduced
resolved
sparked
spearheaded
spoke
succeeded
supervised
surpassed
transferred
unified

Adverbs
accurately
attentively
creatively
efficiently
intelligently
inventively
quickly
responsibly
successfully
uniquely
effectively

University of Missouri-Columbia Career Services

The Real You @Work

Section 3: Your Work History & Experience

Your Work History

This is where you'll want to write out your work history and work *experience* in as much detail as possible. You'll want to capture all **functions, highlights and achievements**. Don't edit or diminish anything. You want to build as comprehensive a picture as possible, so that you can have the best chance to identify all you have to offer *and* most enjoyed!

This is also where your subconscious comes in. There may be things you've forgotten that over time, you'll be prompted to remember.

Note: Though we've provided some pages to record your initial reflections, you can see this layout is meant to be integrated in a larger notebook divided into sections as you think through your work journey.

This is also where you begin to identify your **professional brand story**.

Side Bar | Professional Branding

You may or may not be familiar with the term branding it comes from the marketing field and was first introduced as a way to view yourself professionally by Tom Peters. This article, *The Brand Called You*, in INC magazine published years ago created a new dimension for professional development: https://www.fastcompany.com/28905/brand-called-you

The article was followed up with Tom's book **Brand You**, which I recommend you add to your professional library.

Professional branding can be described as follows…
A professional brand can be a subset of your personal brand. It can include many of your personal characteristics such as how you interact with others your knowledge and how you work in a business environment.

A professional brand can help you:

- clearly define who you are to others – in a way that makes you distinct
- explain what makes you great
- demonstrate why you should be hired
- communicate your reputation and value to an employer
- distinguish yourself as a capable, trustworthy and skilled candidate

- create a consistent and credible image of yourself
- showcase your skills, values and personality
- creating memorable experiences and positive emotions for all you serve

Where to start and what to consider …

⇨ Define your purpose, overriding sense of personal mission.

⇨ Construct your personal narrative - write a bio as if it were a marketing piece.

⇨ Communicate your Brand Story – articulate what kind of professional you are

⇨ Socialize your brand - use social media to express brand expertise, e.g. write articles, comment on posts, offer to be on a podcast. LinkedIn is an essential place to present your brand with a variety of mediums.

Note: Make sure to reevaluate and adjust your brand. This is an important component of ongoing career management.

✍ *Notes*

My Work History Overview

Work History cont…

< My Core Industry Capabilities & Skills>

Next, from your work history/experience do the following…

Thinking through the lens of your experience, answer these questions:

1. What & where did you demonstrate that you were capable of, specific functions (skills/capabilities) that are job specific.
2. Could learn with little to no previous experience (aptitude).
3. What areas did you demonstrate a firm skill, competency or expertise?
4. What work did you do that gave you a meaningful level of enjoyment / satisfaction?

Note:

- Writing out your experience might also prompt you to go back and review your previous base (core) skills/capabilities list.
- If you have an existing resume, do the above (go back and review) on your resume as well. You might gain some interesting insights.

Core industry skills evaluation cont…

Core industry skills evaluation cont…

Highlights & Achievement Guide

I have often found one of the most neglected aspects of career planning and management is *tracking & documenting* achievements *and* more specifically, <u>*quantifying*</u> the results of those achievements with **dollars, percentages and numbers**.

Your ability to do this really puts meat on the bones of what you've contributed and the value you bring. Those dollars, percentages and numbers, <u>amplifies the context</u> in which you achieved them and gives enhanced meaning to your actions.

All of this **makes a stronger case for your value.** Dollars, percentages, and numbers provide tangible proof that you indeed provide a *return on your compensation* beyond just being an employee, but as a true individual contributor and business partner.

This can position you for higher compensation for raises and negotiating starting salary points when interviewing. Think of the value of being able to do this and the money gained compounded over time…a lot more money in your pocket and for your future!

On the worksheet are examples of where to begin. Additionally, here are a few examples:

- Saved $100,000 in 1 quarter through a savings initiative
- Found a process error that netted $250,000 in yearly savings
- 98% retention of my team over 2 years
- Sales increase of $50,000 in one month
- Maintained a 9.8 customer satisfaction rating over the past 12 months

You get the point.

Of note: I'll be introducing something called **Performance Tracker** tool which will help do the above. Whether you use it or your Career Journal, you need to *consistently* track your activity so that you can quantify your contributions and value delivered.

Quantifying Achievements

Use the items listed below to stimulate your thinking in assessing your accomplishments/ achievements during the course of your work experience. On a separate sheet of paper describe each in detail (For a greater scope, include other areas of your life, such as volunteer work or personal projects.) This truly becomes your bio or history of the value you've delivered over time.

- Saved x amount of $
- Designed and implemented
- Improved productivity
- Reduced turnover
- Recruited and trained
- Developed budgets
- Reduced time allocations
- Planned & executed moves
- Revised organization plans
- Directed engagements
- Responsible for_________________
- Evaluated performance
- Minimized client complaints
- Enhanced community relations
- Improved product quality
- Set new goals and objectives
- Devised new strategies or processes
- Staffed….
- Designed ________________goals and objectives
- Organized and directed
- Recovered_____% of uncollectible receivables
- Designed new schedules
- Eliminated obsolete
- Discovered
- Planned and developed

Quantifying Achievements – cont….

Pulling it All Together

Here's your chance to integrate the work you've done so far. From your previous findings choose the most important elements from these core categories and place them here. You're being asked to narrow down the best of what you've discovered.

Your Through Line	Your Core Values	Key Attributes	Skills, Capabilities Talent, Attributes	Achievements Highlights

Your Professional Story – Your Bio

Next: Write a first draft bio that includes the elements from the summary categories. Don't be concerned about it being perfect. This is a draft. It's practice in combining. This will then be used as a source for your interviews, resume and LinkedIn profile.

Though there Is a bit of room here, I recommend grabbing several sheets of paper and free hand-writing your first draft. This approach will help, should you be interviewing. In your mind, you are creating your brand narrative which will be easier to share when asked.

Tip: Another view to consider in writing this bio is to think of it as a marketing document. You are marketing yourself and your professional brand.

The Real You @Work

Section 4: Career Management

Successful Career Management

Now that you've made a first attempt at constructing your portfolio, what comes next?

Next is *creating the habit* of **active career management**. To achieve this, it's best done as an ongoing practice *embedded* in your weekly and quarterly job activities. We've created a blueprint to guide your actions and a 4-page worksheet – The Performance Tracker – to use on a weekly basis.

The Distinct Leader Blueprint for Individual Contributors | A Guide to Successful Career Management
Mindset: Distinct leadership: is intentional, deliberate, strategic, customized. It is not based on a title, but on an individual's authentic, unique contribution. It goes beyond seeing oneself as an employee, but a valuable, distinct business partner.

Stage 3| Accelerate > Disciplined, strategic continuous improvement *(Level 2 - Career management)*	**7/ Refine** Plan to improve execution & output for continuous improvement, effectiveness for organizational impact - incresed value delivered	**8/ Collect** Continuously **collect** organizational intel - to expand impact, expand vision, plan next org. Move Collect org contacts & allys	**9/ Strategic reach & growth** Refine vision & job description, map out areas of next stage growth, contribution, value
Stage 2| Adjust > Create & Use a Performance Tracker *(Level 1 - Career management)*	**4/ Translate** Your strategic plan into tactical action; into daily-weekly activities	**5/ Assign to Time** Create a Time Map - lay out "when will I accomplish these" roadmap to ensure focus, self-accountability = execution success/ integrate into daily/weekly calendar	**6/ Assess Weekly** Self Debrief: What was accomplished, how did my roadmap work; what happened?, what did I learn about myself & others? What value did I deliver? How can I quantitate activity in $, %, #s
Stage 1| Assess > Create a Career/Brand Portfolio (Career planning - foundation)	**1/ Examine** Who am I - What do I bring to the table to contribute= Personal Branding *Activities:* Vision Values Attributes GPS (Guiding Principle statement)	**2/ Identify** - How will I lead/influence/ fulfill my unique vision via my role? *Activity:* Re-write/ customize your job description incorporating information resulting from block 1	**3/ Craft** A strategic plan answering the question: How will I conduct, express myself, uniquely contribute... based on my updated (customized) job description? How will I strategically insert myself (vision, values, attributes, gps) into my job role.

Note: Compiling a career portfolio is what Stage 1: Block #1. **The Performance Tracker** tool helps you to systematically implement the remainder of the building blocks. As you make its use a habit, it *automates* your career management while also promoting peak job performance. **It's performance management *and* career management all in one!**

Successful career planning & management means…

- Being purposeful and strategic in your job performance
- Staying connected to your personal why
- Being mindful of the skills you're developing, the capabilities and capacity you're growing
- Documenting that journey
- Positioning yourself for promotions and raises sourced from that documentation
- Looking for opportunities to grow knowing it will serve you now and in the future. (*Example*: If you know you will soon be ready to make a change, start scoping out your next move. Find out what's needed and use your current role to boost those qualities, skills, knowledge as you prepare to exit.
- Voluntarily getting input from others to fill your blind spots for areas of growth or potential

Documenting is Essential

You can see from the list above that keeping track of what's happening by way of recording, journaling, documenting, logging - whatever you wish to call it - is a must!

So, whether you use our tool or another, please make sure that you don't leave all that you do and the value you deliver to your memory. Keep track of your work. Keep adding to your portfolio at least quarterly. Put a career retreat in your schedule at least semi-annually.

Keep evaluating your professional brand and the journey you want to take, as you craft and playout the story of you!

Career Management Tip

If you are looking to make a change, make sure you have solid ***exit strategy****. As mentioned above, take advantage of your current role to prepare for the next and also make sure you have the finances in place for the transition. Financial planning is an essential factor in successful career management.*

Next Up > An introduction to The Performance Tracker Tool, a unique form of career and performance management

Weekly Career Management – The Ultimate Key to Success

If you really want to set yourself apart and make the most of your career opportunities, do these 2 things:

1. Take active 100% responsibility for your "performance" every week.
2. Marry your career management with your performance management.

Now that you've crafted a first draft of your core Career Portfolio, you'll want to verify your findings through your current work experience and *continue to add* to its contents.

I've created a resource to do just that. As referenced earlier, it's called **The Performance Tracker** – The Ultimate Tool for Career & Performance Success.

This section includes the complete explanation of its origin, the benefits to you and the process when using it. There are also supporting videos on YouTube (look for the Career Playlist) and on my website to help as well – www.joanncorley.com.

Everything you need to apply the process is included in this handbook. However, if you like using it – you can:

- Email me for a master copy of the 4-page tool – joann@joanncorley.com
- buy the workbook on Amazon which includes 6 months of planning including monthly and quarterly.

Career Tip:
Develop business acumen –
see yourself as a business partner

The Distinct Leader

The Distinct Leader Performance Tracker

The Most Unique, Innovative Career & Performance Management Resource You'll Come Across

The Back Story

It's been an interesting 25 plus years in the professional development space. Suffice it to say, I've seen a lot.

As my business has grown beyond my core expertise in human resources, so has my focus on leadership and management. I've observed and worked with *thousands* of folks across North America and most recently globally through my LinkedIn courses.

The breath and duration of this experience has given me a *very distinct* view of the overall strengths and weakness of many leaders and managers as well as the professional development industries that serve them.

What's been downright painful is observing the continuous weaknesses not being addressed by the new generation of HR, leadership and management development industries.

There are 3 areas in particular of concern, 2 of which I'll address now:

1. Performance management
2. Career planning and management
3. The lack of effectiveness in leadership

As you think about those 3, you can probably see they are connected. So, I've been working to address these simply and simultaneously, while addressing a few other needs as well.

Hold Up! So far, you've been referencing leaders and managers. Some of you might be thinking, "Well, I'm not either." Well here is my belief. Whether you hold a formal title or not everyone is a leader and manager in some way. Though without specific title, we influence results with ourselves and others through leadership and management behaviors.

Ok, back to addressing the top 2 areas of concern.

Area #1: Performance Management
In general, it's a hot mess.

There is soooo much I could say about this, but I won't because I want to keep my blood pressure down. I'll summarize it this way, most employee performance management practices *for all levels*, even with the most sophisticated software are not particularly useful, mostly meaningless and therefore waste tremendous amounts of time and money.

Notice I did say "in general". There are some that are useful…to varying degrees. Though many ask is the time spent using them netting any real value?

So, if what I'm saying is even remotely true, we can conclude that many employees' careers and compensation - both of which have long term ripple effects - are being left victim to the whole faulty shebang - the design, how it's used and who is using it, etc. Ugh!

And…if you're one of those users - a leader/manager - it's a reflection of and impact on your effectiveness.

I'm gonna go "O.G." for a moment. I've been employed by some very successful companies where the performance management practices and software we use today **did not exist**. Two were on the INC 500 list, one of which was #1. It was the relationships and company culture that drove employee engagement, retention and profits.

Let that sink in...companies were highly successful *without* them!! Awhhhh simpler times!

#2: Career Planning & Management

Reactionary vs. Deliberate

Let's just admit it, for most, career planning and management doesn't exist. Most career action is reactionary. I want to change jobs; I create a resume.

A resume that is, in theory, supposed to represent the best of you - your experience and what you have to offer...all on 1 page.

Sounds kind of absurd really. The best of you condensed to a few lines crammed on usually 1 sheet of paper.

But oh... you are sooo much more than that! Additionally, in the process of the cramming and text finagling, you have to call up the best of your experience from the deep recesses of your memory, which I know at least for me is spotty at best.

There's got to be a better way!

First, I'd like to recommend that you take action today, this week to begin active career planning and management. Whether you use my resources or someone else's, commit to embedding this practice into your work life.

Second, if you don't have a current resource at your fingertips, I suggest considering mine.

My idea

These things continued gnawing at me, I just felt compelled to do something. So, one day I got an idea that connects career planning and management to performance management. I wanted to create something that simultaneously addressed both in an innovative way.

Innovative means combining, tweaking or adjusting something for better use and outcomes for the user. And so, I started asking myself these questions:

- What if we integrated career planning and management into performance management, by first seeing and using performance management differently?
- What if we looked at performance management through the lens of contribution, value and results rather than *subjective* ratings of qualities or competencies?
- What if there was a tool where an individual planned and directed their own performance management through strategic execution of their job description while also seeing it is as career management?
- What if this resource was also flexible? One that offered a core framework of integrating career and performance management, but still could be used in other ways.

After considering these questions, I came up with a resource that meets all the criteria. It's a performance tracking system – designed through the lens of behavioral neuroscience - that cultivates and documents **successful execution of a job role** in *weekly cycles.* Activity and results are self-monitored in real-time which also serves as an on-going form of career management.

One of my favorite parts of this resource is the significant benefit to leaders/managers. It empowers and positions employees as true "individual *contributors*" and collaborative partners. If you incorporate this tool in your team, you'll flip the script on what it means to manage people.

With built in accountability, it empowers them to self-manage as you facilitate and support their success, *while* getting the needed outcomes for your team, department or business unit. To use Stephen Covey's adage, it truly is a "win-win".

For many, career planning and management and performance management are truly 2 *perpetual* pain points. That's why I am on a mission to successfully address them both!

So, here's what I'm setting out to do:

The Mission

- Mitigate the effect of deeply flawed performance management practices that adversely affect career and compensation for all employees, at all levels
- Help people learn how to use their everyday work experience to successfully manage their careers and professional brand as an offset
- Achieve greater levels of personal confidence & job satisfaction (stay connected to their why)
- Reduce performance management stressors for all parties
- In general, making it easier to lead and manage
- Modernize how performance management seeing it from a holistic point of view rather than industrial age thinking
- Have a solution that *anyone* can afford

The above is my core mission. This resource also has additional benefits such as:

- boosting employee engagement and retention
- better talent management, including coaching
- improved team culture and collaboration
- …and more!

| The Solution |

The Name*:* The Distinct Leader Performance Tracker for Next Level Career Success
The Approach*:* a 5-step system – *handwritten* - conducted in *weekly* cycles:

Plan it – Map it - Manage it – Measure it – Mention it.

The approach and supporting tools provide a structured system:

1. *Structure:* Structure creates an intentional framework providing boundaries from which to act.

   Benefit: creates a sense of familiarity and control that can reduce your stress levels and help you feel more in control of your time and life in general.

2. *A System*: A set of principles and procedures

   Benefit: a system provides a *continuous feedback loop* and with this approach using behavioral neuroscience to provide opportunities for continuous improvement. So, our system promotes focus (activates the RAS - reticular activating system in the brain) and helps develop rhythms and habits which produce more predictable results with less energy.

3. *The Gauge:* A gauge is something this is used to measure.

   Benefit: Since we're measuring contribution and valued results rather than qualities and competencies, we need a way to measure in concrete, tangible ways (objective vs. subjective). So, with this system, we're using a universally familiar gauge and that is time. Time, as the base gauge, is the easiest and most logical to use because that's where performance practically plays out.

There are 2 essential elements to this system - time & writing by hand.

A Few Thoughts About Time > Time is Where it All Happens!

I see time as a business partner - even a life partner. It is an essential asset and resource to having the life you want. It is the **truth teller** of your (or anyone's) effectiveness, competency and performance.

	Sunday	Monday	Tuesday	Wednesday	Thursday	Friday	Saturday
7:00 a.m.							
8:00							
9:00							
10:00							
11:00							
12:00							
1:00 p.m.							
2:00							
3:00							
4:00							
5:00							
6:00							
7:00							
8:00							
9:00							
10:00							

Time is the fundamental gauge we use in any business from accounting to human resources and that's why I think it's taken for granted. It's naturally embedded in our existence.

And yet, when we use it with intention, we can reap enormous benefits. For example, if you want to change any behavior or develop a new habit, time is typically used to track progress.

Tracking our action and effort via time is a common approach. Time serves as the tool, the reality check, and therefore **the ultimate coach**. That's pretty powerful....and for all that, it costs nothing! It's all free!! Pretty cool!

So, it's a natural measuring and tracking resource to use for career and performance management. The way in which we're using it also offers tremendous additional benefits.

By using the performance tracker system as designed, you'll;

- **Leverage and grow key skills of execution** such as strategic thinking & planning - considering best actions and results by asking the question, "How can

I be the most effective for the job role?" with benefits to the professional brand & career in mind. This boosts ownership and personal accountability.

- **Document successful execution** (going beyond the preverbal "to do" list) – documented time use gauges actions and outcomes.
- **Cultivate *continuous* improvement** - using *weekly cycles* to assess and plan, you'll be generating your own improvement. In essence, you're developing the habit of improving.

- **Identify & document** *ongoing* financial contribution and value

- Be **incorporating human behavior science which** fosters *sustainable* performance improvement.

- And since it's **driven by the individual contributor** and supported by the team and direct report, it's considered a bottom up vs. top down approach to performance management.

Why Hand-Written?

Since our approach and tools are designed using neuro and behavioral science, using the tool and process in a hand-written format is essential to *maximize* the design. Technology is robbing us, not only of brain development, but best brain usage.

Please see the bonus article at the end for a complete explanation.

Reframing How We See Performance

Usage:

Mindset - as we mentioned, everyone is a leader – so this performance tool promotes a strong, valuable professional brand and impact - whether you have a formal title or not. Additionally, there is a mindset shift from "employee" to *contributor* and **business partner**.

Let's look at what the key terms mean:
Contributor: someone who gives their time or effort in order to help achieve something.
Partner/Collaborator: working together to achieve results

Mantra: Everything *I choose* to do serves my current *and* future success.

This mindset suggests that you want to contribute as much value as you can because that it's in your best interest to do so. We call this "ROC" - return on compensation. In its purest form, compensation is an investment on an expected, needed return.

Motive - your mindset and mantra then form your motive. It is your *personal why* - why you do what you do and therefore fuels your motivation. If you stay connected to your why, you'll continually be motivated.

Here is our systematic 5 step method for performance and career management. We gauge and ***plan success*** *in weekly cycles.*

As you read about the 5-Step process, note the pages used in our system as indicated on the following page. At the back of this handbook is the full-size version of each page for you to copy (4-pages for each week). You can also request a master copy or get 6 months' worth via the book on Amazon which also includes monthly and quarterly planning.

Plan It

The Distinct Leader | Performance Tracker
Plan It, Map It, Manage It, Measure It, Mention It

Plan for Week #

Guiding Mindset/Mantra=>

Strategic Plan Statement=> Overall Desires for This Week

This Week's **Essential Actions** -To Do List:

Targeted Results for This Week - *What I'd like to achieve*

TDL | Performance Tracker - Rockin My Story - 1

Map It – Manage It

The Distinct Leader | Performance Tracker
Plan It, Map It, Manage It, Measure It, Mention It

Time Blocks	Monday	Tuesday	Wednesday	Thursday	Friday	Saturday
8						
9						
10						
11						
12						
1						
2						
3						
4						
5						

Misc. Notes:

TDL | Performance Tracker - Rockin My Story - 2

Measure It

The Distinct Leader | Performance Tracker
Plan It, Map It, Manage It, Measure It, Mention It

Charting My Impact: Identifying My Value Chain / Results / Ripple Effect

The Ripple Effect - Impact Map Template
Enterprise Overview
Looking beyond the results = What's the *ripple effect?*...the extended value at cost? (both short & long term)

My Contribution

Circle touch-points and impact *across* the enterprise

Key Collaborators:	**Operational Performance:**	**Customer Impact:**	**Company Branding:**
Direct report	Productivity/timely	Satisfaction	Talent
Team members	Timing -	Retention	Attraction/acquisition
Internal	opportunity cost	Increase sales	Client attraction
departments	Quality	New or upgraded	Investor Attraction /
External vendors	Improved revenue	products/services	VC-Stockholders
External Partners	opportunities		

Anything to include - unique to your organisation?

And...
Anything relative regarding distinct personal brand

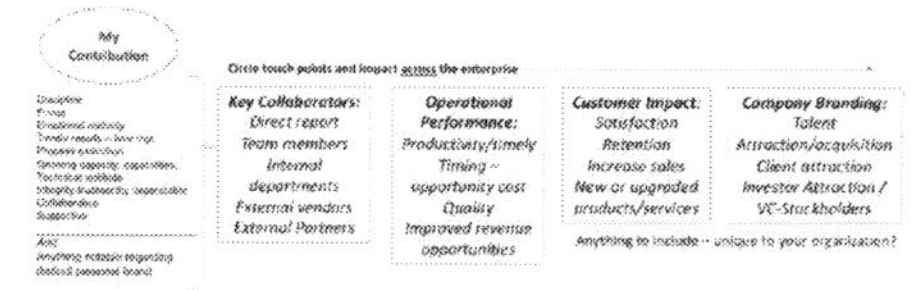

How did my activity and results impact these key areas?

TDL | Performance Tracker - Rockin My Story - 3

Mention It

The Distinct Leader | Performance Tracker
Plan It, Map It, Manage It, Measure It, Mention It

Weekly Summary - My Story This Week
My Wins...

What did I learn about myself, others, process, organization, other stakeholders? What will I adjust next week? What will I mention?

TDL | Performance Tracker - Rockin My Story - 4

Summary: 5 Steps for Strategic Career & Performance Management

*Note your mindset here…you are moving beyond just "doing your job description or to-do list…you are **planning and activating weekly success**.*

1/ Plan it: From your overall "to do list" **-** determine what needs to be done this week, considering the A priorities (absolutely needs to get done), most important, most impact. If you use a running to do list, it's good to take these off and *only view what's absolutely needed for the week*. This helps minimize overwhelm and dial-in your focus and energy.

2/ Map it: This is where strategic thinking and planning takes place. You'll be creating an execution map by laying out *all* your activity (including your "to-do" items) on your calendar. Consider how you ideally want to execute them. This includes estimating how long something will take or how much time you're willing to allot for each.

Once you map it, *reality has been applied*. You'll be able to have a *complete view* of what can be realistically executed in a week and where you've assigned your priorities. This also helps build time awareness.

Note: Beside planning for success**, the act of strategic mapping** also helps you develop 3 key time/performance management skills:
- Time estimation - learning how long you think it takes to do an activity/task
- Time blocking - planning when is the best time to do them
- Time awareness - how long activities are *actually* taking

3/ Manage it: This means managing the day-to-day execution of your plan, knowing things will pop up, unforeseen issues may occur. So, those events and related decisions have to be managed.

Think about your decision-making in how you're handling those events compared against what's been previously mapped. This is priority and execution management which has a direct impact on your performance and getting needed results.

Your map now serves as your *ultimate* decision-making guide and performance coach.

4/ Measure it: Measuring includes several actions:

A. **Assessing your progress -** you want to become "results-oriented".

B. **Quantify your activity and results** to determine the value you're providing.

This is one of my favorite parts (and which few people do). Many times, when I'm helping folks construct a resume, I ask how they can *quantify* their work, accomplishments or highlights. Quantify means translating activity and outcomes into dollars, percentages, and/or numbers. This gives concrete meaning and context to the results of their activity. *E.g.* I saved the company X amount of $s. We finished ahead of schedule which saved the team 25% of time allotted.

Key point: You can see how doing this in real time is helpful in maintaining a current portfolio. Imagine trying to do this justice, off the top of your head from memory.

A Unique Opportunity

We not only help clients quantify their contributions; we teach them how to identify something we call "their **value chain**". **Everyone has one!** When working through the lens of behavior you can see *every behavior*/action has a ripple effect. We help folks identify and financially quantify that.

Do you know your "ripple effect"?

This ongoing practice cultivates business acumen, which comes in quite handy when you are discussing raises. Being able to do this, best positions you - as realistically as possible – in your current job or also when interviewing. All of this is built into our weekly tool!

C. **Acknowledge what's been completed** is another practice of measuring and healthy performance/career management. We call it *success tracking*. We see success not just from the view of - for example – an entire project being completed - but *the completion of micro-steps* as well. Without completion of the micros, the macro would not be complete.

This is particularly important for those who only see what's not finished vs. what has been. That type of thinking - seeing what's not complete - drains energy and motivation which can lead to unnecessary burnout.

Also, if you diminish your work in your own eyes, you won't represent yourself well to others. **You *must* be your best advocate**! Tracking and documenting your work helps you do this with confidence and clarity. It also embeds a psychology of success.

By the way, this is part of the *psychology of completion*. Completeness generates energy and incompleteness drains energy. A sense of incompleteness is like constantly having a "monkey on your back" from which you just can't get relief. That nagging weight can be relentless. You could be doing great work, providing tons of value…but don't see it or *feel* it!

So, for some, we have to **intentionally see - pay attention -** to completion by *creating the practice,* the habit of reviewing what has been done and even lingering there for a moment (this is me) allowing oneself to *fully feel* that good feeling of completion *and* seeing the value of it. We recommend doing this at the end of each day. And sometimes, I occasionally build in some type of reward.

So, measuring and acknowledging progress - even the smallest amount - is essential to managing
your motivation, sense of satisfaction, confidence, sense of relevance, and value.
These are all elements of performance and career management.

Q: How are you managing the experience of your day to day work?

Here's another example. Have you ever had a busy day and ended it thinking, "What the heck did I get done today?" Assessing your activity, seeing the value of it, even if you've taken a complete detour from your map that day, is an example of why this practice is so important.

You did spend time doing *something!* So, identify and record what it was, why it mattered and how it served the overall vision or strategic plan. And if it didn't, this will create the opportunity to self-correct, process improve for the next day or week.

You can see where daily practice related to this example is particularly useful because you don't want to fall down "a rabbit hole" and have your whole week hijacked.

So, adopting this daily habit, can consistently reduce days like that, incrementally improving your effectiveness. That's why we call **your time map your self-development coach.** It helps you see and deal with your truth and level of discipline.

5/ Mention it: *Voluntarily* provide your results to your direct report, so he/she will *never be in the dark* of the value you are delivering. And mentioning goes beyond sharing activities, but also quantified results. Adopt the principle - "Leave no doubt." No more surprise, blind-sided performance reviews…ok, well maybe at least hopefully mitigated.

Career Tip Actively manage your brand perception…

Key Point

As a collaborative partner, when this is built into your regular workflow - you initiate conversations and *shape your professional brand narrative* **as you go** rather than leaving the perception of your performance to a faulty process and/or unskilled manager only to be discussed or recognized every 6 months or so. This is an essential element of brand and career management.

And even if your company has exceptional performance management, the use of these practices coupled with our tracker tools/process, will provide a current, ongoing record of your experience from which you can source for formal performance reviews, constructing the best resume as well as providing valuable content for interviews. You'll have a hard time choosing *the best stuff* rather than struggling to "figure out" what to say. That's a great problem to have!

Bringing It Full Circle

Now that you've learned the 5-step system. Let's draw these conclusions.

First > Time management is performance management when approached through this strategic lens…it is your performance partner.

Second > Performance management is career management.

Combing the use of activity & time tracking, performance, and career management is a holistic approach which provides tremendous value not only for the individual but for the employer. It's an approach that can transform how you see and *experience* work.

It deals with the whole of you – it combines your aspirations with how you operate day-to-day… your thoughts, feelings, motivation, energy, spirit rather than just having just a job and being assessed from a narrow, fluctuating view of certain characteristics.

Summary of Benefits

Ultimately, the goal of **The Distinct Leader Performance Tracker System** is to *help you:*

- Cultivate *continuous* confidence and self-value
- Maintain a strong leadership mindset (whether you have an official title or not...knowing those who are delivering value are leaders)
- Transform your approach to work/your role beyond a basic job description and the proverbial to-do list, but to contribution & value
- Develop and fine-tune your strategic thinking, planning, and decision-making
- Stay ruthlessly focused
- Feed and maintain your personal motivation
- Create the disciplines of *successful, effective* execution
- Master habits of self-coaching & self-management
- Build a powerful professional narrative

Which will in turn...

- ➢ provide opportunities for greater success
- ➢ supplies a continuous, real-time record of your work so that you can have more informed conversations, strongly and competently advocating for yourself with whatever performance management practices your company currently has in place.
- ➢ help you better manage your career and professional brand over the course of your working life
- ➢ position you for the best possibilities at each stage of your career
- ➢ boost your earning potential. Remember the value of your earnings over time is compounded, so you want to earn the most at each opportunity.

In summary, the whole point of this handbook is to help you determine your best actions, deliver high-value results, document your success along the way and decipher your financial contribution equal to and beyond your return on compensation.

What you've read or heard today can be executed and achieved without us. However, if you want to save time and ramp up quickly consider using our system, tools and support for just a few dollars.

It's the ultimate resource for you to feel more confident and in control while transforming your career and performance.

One Final Note

As you know it is my desire to re-imagine performance management for the modern age. As I see it holistically, I imagine it as an opportunity to craft an incredible story…your story.

It's a success story of impact - someone making their mark. The narrative describes how someone marries their personal vision, sense of purpose or mission, skills and talents with the needs of an enterprise and through that makes a unique contribution.

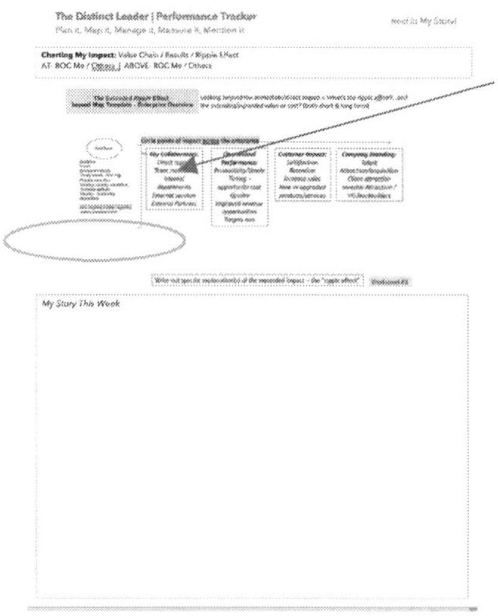

There is a section on our template just for that - a place to record your story. **We invite you to transform your weekly performance into your career success narrative.** Each week is considered a chapter to add. You can even consider your time map your story board. Cool huh!

Please remember, your boss <u>will have</u> a narrative of your performance. Effective performance and career management is influencing that narrative as much as possible. Boy does that take performance management way beyond let me rate you a 4 on communication.

Elevate how you see your work! Inspire yourself and others! *Starting today,* what is and will be your story (your narrative to yourself and others)? Though today may be partially written, as Natasha Bedingfield said, “The rest is still unwritten.”

Decide who you are and do it with power and purpose! Rock your story!

|> Recommended Actions

- Check out the complete **walk-through video** of the tracker tool and explanation of its strategic design. – go to www.joanncorley.com
- Reminder full 4-page sheets are in the back
- Contact me for any questions: joann@joanncorley.com
- Consider using it in your organization – offer internal rollouts of cohorts with teams, departments.
- Get it! Use it! Experience its Impact!

| Bonus Article

Using the Neuroscience of Writing to Improve Employee Performance

Introduction | The Neuroscience of Writing

Writing by hand is a skill that has been around for centuries. However, with the rise of technology, it has become less common for people to write by hand. Instead, they use keyboards and touchscreens to communicate. But what impact does this shift have on the brain?

The Science

When we write by hand, we engage large regions of the brain responsible for thinking, language, healing, and working memory which includes the motor cortex (this controls movement), and the somatosensory cortex, which processes sensory information from the hand. Engaging multiple brain regions helps to strengthen neural connections and improve overall brain function.

Summary:

When you write, all parts of your brain are actively engaged. Thanks to the brain's neuroplasticity, it can grow and change over time.

The more you write, the more your brain responds by establishing new neural connections within these regions.

Benefits to Writing

Cultivate Positivity: Writing is good for keeping one's gray matter sharp and may even influence how we think, as in "more positively."

Reduced Stress: Writing by hand can also be a great way to reduce stress, anxiety and even mild depression. The act of writing can be meditative and calming. Writing activates the imagination generating pictures and movies in our mind which stimulates the release of neurotransmitters (brain chemicals). The *added benefit* is successfully reducing stress can promote healing and improve sleep

Writing can literally change or shift the chemistry in your brain.

Improves Learning & Comprehension: Research has shown that writing by hand can also help with learning and comprehension. Studies have found that students who take notes by hand perform better on exams and have a deeper understanding of the material. This is because writing by hand forces the brain to process information differently.

Boosts Focus: Writing also help you focus your thoughts and clear your mind. It keeps the brain sharp.

Fosters Deep & Creative Thinking: Making writing a regular habit has been shown to increase creative and critical thinking. It deepens thinking by activating and tuning into the subconscious. Also, when you write by hand, you are forced to slow down and think more deeply about what you are writing. This can lead to more creative ideas and insights.

Increases Memory: Results show that the brain in both young adults and children is much more active when writing by hand than when typing on a keyboard. **"The use of pen and paper gives the brain more 'hooks' to hang your memories on.** In one study, participants who wrote notes by hand were able to remember the information better than those who typed their notes on a computer. This promoted improved retention and recall.

Interesting Tidbits:
Using technology has led to a decline in the amount of time people spend writing by hand, which can have negative consequences on brain development.

With electronic devices, people can easily edit and delete their writing, which can lead to a lack of focus and attention to detail. This can have a negative impact on the brain's ability to process information and retain it for the long term.

Using Writing in Employee Performance Management

When considering all the effects and benefits to the brain when writing and since the brain is the origin of performance, why not use this science to cultivate improved employee performance.

The Habit of Planning & Recording

We've all experienced the value or even downfall created by habits. They run our lives - if we are truthful with ourselves. And so, why not adopt that same power applying it to employee performance. Why not intentionally create habits that power the outcomes we want to achieve?

A habit is an embedded neuropathy way that generates an *automated* behavior. An automated behavior is cool in that, we don't have to think about it, don't have to force ourselves to do it and therefore requires very little if any energy.

So, if we used performance management strategically to create targeted habits - both for individuals *and* teams - we would be <u>*continuously cultivating*</u> the performance / behaviors *and* results we want.

How? Combining Writing with Strategic Performance Management

The easiest way to do this is by having an employee institute the habit of planning and recording. If we created a tool that strategically guides this activity prompted on a continuous basis - ideally through weekly cycles - this could be achieved. And so, we've done that! It's the Distinct Leader Performance Tracker.

Additionally, as a bonus, we added one more layer. What if the tool could also be used for active career management? What if we combined performance management and career management within the use of one tool…all driven and controlled by the employee? This is how our tool can be used!

Though surprisingly simple, the layout and design of our innovative tool incorporates all the neuroscience benefits of writing.

| About the Author |

JoAnn R. Corley is a globally recognized leadership, management, HR, speaker and advisor. She has been named consistently to several top 50 Global Leadership & HR thought leader and influencer lists.

Her mission is to help individuals and companies cultivate effective leaders by helping them connect to their authentic power - which she believes lies in the best of humanity. She calls that the "human quotient".

Her overriding business philosophy is "when we are our best human selves, we will be the best leaders our organizations and enterprises need". She believes we are entering a new era of corporate leadership where personal power expressed through relationships is profoundly more effective than positional, authoritative power. This belief, her fundamental business philosophy, and expertise in working with human behavior science are embedded in her pioneering leadership development work.

In her 25+ years career, she has delivered thousands of workshops, along with keynotes in every major city and state in the U.S., a unique distinction. Her in-person and online workshops have included leaders and managers from a variety of Fortune 500 & 1000, private and publicly traded companies, as well as governmental agencies. *Partial list:* US Marshals, US Army, Microsoft, The City of Chicago, Flowers Foods, Atlanta Federal Reserve, University of Iowa, Duke Energy, ESPN, Yale Club of New York City, Chicago White Sox, University of Georgia, Clemson University, 3M, Kum Academy-Dubai and NASA to name a few.

She has also been quoted or featured in a variety of radio shows, print and on-line media including NBC News, Huffington Post, Monster.com, Smerconish.com, Harvard Business Review, SHRM National, HR Magazine and Management Business Daily.

She has written multiple books (see Amazon Author page) and has 2 highly acclaimed LinkedIn Learning courses on managing employee performance.

Where to find her on Social Media: Twitter, LinkedIn, TikTok, Threads, Instagram, Facebook
Website: www.joanncorley.com Blog: www.joanncorleyspeaks.com
E-coach monthly: www.thedistinctleader.com
Amazon author link: https://www.amazon.com/stores/author/B004HGQKZ2

| Contact JoAnn |

I want so much for you to have a satisfying, successful career – to make the impact you were born to make… I've created other resources to compliment this book.

First, since you've purchased the handbook, if you'd like to have the entire book in a pdf format, or even a word doc so that you can break it a part and put it in a physical notebook, email me and I'll be happy to send it to you.

Other Resources:

Master pages of the Performance Tracker – to follow

YouTube Channel – There is **playlist** dedicated to career planning & management

Subscribe to my monthly e-coach: InFocus – www.thedistinctleader.com

Email me: joann@joanncorley.com

Wishing you wild success!

JoAnn

Plan for Week #

Guiding Mindset/Mantra=>

Strategic Plan Statement=> Overall Desires for This Week

This Week's **Essential Actions** -To Do List:

Targeted Results for This Week – *What I'd like to achieve*

Time Blocks	Monday	Tuesday	Wednesday	Thursday	Friday	Saturday
8						
9						
10						
11						
12						
1						
2						
3						
4						
5						

Misc. Notes:

Charting My Impact: Identifying My Value Chain / Results / Ripple Effect

The Ripple Effect – Impact Map Template
Enterprise Overview

Looking beyond the results = What's *the ripple effect*?...the extended value or cost? (both short & long term)

My Contribution

Discipline
Focus
Emotional maturity
Timely results – time mgt.
Process execution
Growing capacity, capabilities,
Technical aptitude
Integrity-trustworthy dependable
Collaborative
Supportive

Add:
Anything notable regarding distinct personal brand

Circle touch points and impact across the enterprise →

Key Collaborators:	***Operational Performance:***	***Customer Impact:***	***Company Branding:***
Direct report	*Productivity/timely*	*Satisfaction*	*Talent*
Team members	*Timing – opportunity cost*	*Retention*	*Attraction/acquisition*
Internal departments	*Quality*	*Increase sales*	*Client attraction*
External vendors	*Improved revenue opportunities*	*New or upgraded products/services*	*Investor Attraction / VC-Stockholders*
External Partners			

Anything to include – unique to your organization?

How did my activity and results impact these key areas?

Weekly Summary - My Story This Week

My Wins…

What did I learn about myself, others, process, organization, other stakeholders? What will I adjust next week? What will I mention?

Made in the USA
Columbia, SC
21 February 2025

54197444R00050